nal Booklet

C000263469

The JOURNEY
FOR NEW CHRISTIANS

Published 2011 by CWR, Waverley Abbey House,
Waverley Lane, Farnham, Surrey GU9 8EP, UK.
Registered Charity No. 294387.
Registered Limited Company No. 1990308.

For a list of our National Distributors visit
www.cwr.org.uk/distributors

Unless otherwise indicated, all Scripture
references are from the Holy Bible: New
International Version (NIV), copyright © 1973,
1978, 1984 by the International Bible Society.

Concept development, editing, design
and production by CWR

Printed in UK by Nuffield Press

ISBN: 978-1-85345-583-4

DAILY READINGS AND GROUP
DISCUSSION QUESTIONS:
JEFF LUCAS

CWR Applying God's Word
to everyday life and relationships

Contents

THE early days of being a follower of Jesus are often a mixture of wonder, bewilderment, questions and excitement – a strange cocktail! As a new Christian, having determined to turn over the rest of my days to God, my heart was filled with a passionate urgency to live a life that honoured Him. They were heady times, and it was really incredible to discover truths about God that had never previously occurred to me. More than that, learning to walk in faith and friendship with Him was joyful – if, at times, confusing.

Being a Christian is far more than gathering information about God: it's about knowing that we will never be alone again and that He is with us always. An apprentice of Jesus is, first of all, someone who walks with Christ in daily friendship, learning and being discipled by Him.

And so I'm praying that *Life – The Journey for New Christians* will be of real help to you. May you find encouragement and direction as we share these days together. Remember that you are someone who has decided to become a learner – you have not arrived, but are just beginning your journey. When you fall over, get up. When you have questions, ask a trusted friend. When you don't understand, relax and trust. The Christian life is just that – a lifelong pursuit!

And God bless you …

Jeff

PREPARATION FOR GROUP LEADERS

How to use

This resource is designed to include all you will need for six small-group sessions. It comprises six DVD clips, icebreakers, group discussion questions and prayers based on each clip and Bible readings to be used between each session.

1. Watch the DVD clip before the meeting.
2. Use the icebreaker to get people chatting. Select the questions that you think would be most useful for your group to look at. You may want to use them all, depending on the time you have available. We suggest you plan for 30—45 minutes.

THE SESSION

1. Play the DVD clip first and go straight into the icebreaker question.
2. Use the questions you have selected.
3. Move from discussion into prayer. There's a prayer included in the material which you could finish with at the end.
4. Encourage the group to use the daily readings in the days between sessions. The readings expand and build on the topics covered in the DVD. If the group members are not used to daily Bible reading, encourage them to develop this habit. If the group members are already into a routine of Bible reading and prayer each day you might want to discuss how best to work these new readings into their time.
5. You could start the next session by reviewing how the group found the daily readings. What did they learn? Do they have questions to raise? How did God speak?

If using this series on your own:

1. After watching the DVD clip, use the questions for further thought to help you think through the issues involved.
2. Over the following days, use the daily readings which will expand and build on the topics covered in the DVD.
3. You may find it helpful to record what you learn in a notebook or journal.

Session 1
Beginnings –
Under starter's orders

ICEBREAKER:
What is the nicest gift you have ever received?
Think about it – or tell others about it if you are in a group.

FOR GROUP DISCUSSION/FURTHER THOUGHT:
- Why do we sometimes struggle with the truth that God loves us?

- Choices have consequences. What are some of the results of good and bad decisions we make?

- Adults tend to be suspicious of free gifts – why?

- What does it mean for us to turn over our failures to God?

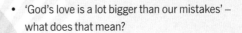

- 'God's love is a lot bigger than our mistakes' – what does that mean?

- How would you tell the 'story' of your own journey with God so far?

- What's the difference between being sad about the wrong we've done, and actually repenting of it?

PRAYER:

Thank You for the free gift
of Your love, Lord.
Help me to surrender
my fears, failures,
hopes and dreams
to You, today.
Amen.

Resources:

Jeff Lucas, *Walking Backwards: Dealing with Guilt* (Milton Keynes: Authentic Publishing, 2010)

THE Bible begins with a fabulous announcement. Genesis is loaded with the biggest news ever. It tells us that we're not accidental, and that planet Earth is not a bauble spinning in space without reason. The words 'In the beginning God created' make up the most explosive sentence in history. And the Creator did not begin His work with a frown of disapproval: everything was declared *good*. In fact, the incredible, amazing, perfect God used Himself to model humanity on – we are made in His image.

And just as the Old Testament opens with news of God at the beginning of everything, so John opens his Gospel with words of God's ongoing care. God is both the Creator and the Rescuer of humanity.

Yet God's big story continues today. God continues to be active in His world – and now, as a follower of Jesus, you have a part in that unfolding story. The picture of Adam and Eve walking around the Garden with God is a good snapshot of what Christianity is. The Bible talks about us 'living by the Spirit', which literally means 'walking around with God' (Gal. 5:16). Of course, we can't see or touch God right now, and recognising His voice is a learned art, but make no mistake – you are not alone. And you never will be again.

Prayer: Thank You, Lord, for this new life – not just of truths and ideas, but a life of walking with You. Lead me today, and always. Amen.

Beginnings

BIG PICTURE
Genesis 1:1–31
John 1:1–18

FOCUS
'God saw all that he had made, and it was very good. And there was evening, and there was morning – the sixth day.'
(Gen. 1:31)

The Bible

begins with

a fabulous

announcement

Freedom and choices

BIG PICTURE
Genesis 3:1–24
Romans 3:22–26

FOCUS
'So the LORD God banished him from the Garden of Eden to work the ground from which he had been taken.'
(Gen. 3:23)

I HAVE officiated at quite a few weddings, and it's always a moment of slight apprehension when both bride and groom are invited to speak up for themselves. 'Will you take this man …?' 'Will you take this woman …?' Momentary tension crackles. Will they go through with it?

No marriage can begin without the vital words 'I will' being spoken. Love is a free choice, and only as each person 'wills' to be wedded to the other can their marriage begin.

In Eden, it all started so well. But God's creation wouldn't be complete if there were no opportunity for decisions. As with marriage, to love someone involves the freedom of choice. We are humans, not puppets or robots. And so God built free will into His creation. And the first humans chose disastrously.

Choices have consequences; and now sin is part of the human condition for us all. We're all sinners at heart, literally (Rom. 3:23). That's the bad news. But there's better news. Christ died for our sins – that includes yours – and now is alive. And, as a new follower of Jesus, you have freely chosen to accept His offer of grace. Whatever bad you've done, it's been forgiven. It is scandalous, but true. That is why the gospel is called the 'good news'. Be glad – you've made the best choice of your life.

Prayer: Lord, I praise You because, whatever my history, I have a wonderful future with You – and that includes today. Amen.

Choices have

consequences

IT HAPPENED again today. Yet another email arrived telling me that I can receive £20 million. I pressed 'Delete'.

Once we reach adulthood, we become increasingly suspicious of free gifts or impossibly good deals, fearing a catch somewhere. But there *is* such a thing as a free *life*, if not a free *lunch*. Trapped in the consequences of living in a sinful cosmos, there was nothing we could do to save ourselves from sin. Just as sin cut Adam and Eve off from God in the Garden, so we find ourselves separated from God. Trying to be good enough to impress God is a little like trying to lift ourselves up by our own shoelaces. It just can't be done.

Enter the rescuing Jesus. He came not only to die on the cross, but also to live the ultimate good life, showing us that we can once again live in friendship with God. He came not just to teach, but also to give us the power to become transformed people, as we 'walk around' with Him each day. As He died on the cross the thick curtain in the Temple was ripped in half, indicating that an 'Access all areas' pass to God is now available to all who want it. And then He was resurrected three days later.

We could do nothing. At the cross, Jesus did it all.

Prayer: Father, I praise You for the work of Jesus. You have done everything for me to live and die in You. We will always be together. Amen.

At the cross

BIG PICTURE
Matthew 27:45–28:10
Romans 5:1–11

FOCUS
'But God demonstrates his own love for us in this: While we were still sinners, Christ died for us.'
(Rom. 5:8)

The kingdom call

BIG PICTURE
Matthew 6:1–34
Colossians 1:1–14

FOCUS
'But seek first his kingdom and his righteousness, and all these things will be given to you as well.'
(Matt. 6:33)

I AM not that close to the royal family. By that, I mean they don't know me at all. I met Prince Philip once (a life-changing experience – for him …!).

Humour aside, I live in the United *Kingdom*, a territory where the reign of Queen Elizabeth extends. But when I first heard this phrase 'the *kingdom of God*', I was terribly confused. The 'kingdom' was the main message of Jesus – but just what is it? It is difficult to think about a kingdom without there being a piece of land associated with it.

When Jesus speaks of the kingdom, He is talking about the sphere of God's rule and influence. As Christians, we are now kingdom 'citizens'. As we seek, each day, to put God's rule first, every part of our lives is affected by our decision to follow Jesus Christ.

Now we have a new purpose and our ambition is to see His kingdom – His rule – widen. Our aim is to push back the darkness of injustice and oppression, as more and more discover the true King of kings: Jesus. We want others to come into this kingdom and discover His loving rule. And, not only that, we discover He is not a distant monarch. As we walk with Him by faith, we get to know Him. This is the kingdom: this is our new priority.

**Prayer: May Your kingdom come, in my life, in the lives of those I love and in the world.
Let me be an agent of Your kingdom. Amen.**

'REPENT!' It's a word that conjures up an image of an odd-looking chap harassing pedestrians as they pass by. In his hand, he holds a sign printed in old-fashioned Gothic script: 'Repent, the end is nigh.' It all seems antiquated and strange.

That's a shame, because repentance is a key to better, healthier days. Repentance is not only about being sorry for sin or even changing our mind about our morals. It's a word that describes us embracing a whole new way of thinking about everything, as we take on board a kingdom value system as followers of Jesus. As we will see tomorrow, this new life really is new and means that we accept God's perspective on the way life should be lived.

And although it does involve being sorry for sin as well, it is more than offering an apology. 'Sorry' is a relatively easy word to say. But being sorry doesn't necessarily mean that we are going to change. We can be sorry for damage we have caused, or because we don't like the pangs of guilt we feel. It is possible to be sorry every day of our lives – and yet continue in the same destructive behaviour. This is what Paul would call 'worldly sorrow'. Real repentance leads to changed thinking and changed living.

Prayer: Change my heart, change my mind, change my desires and motives, that my life and behaviour might be changed today, loving God. Amen.

A whole new way of thinking

BIG PICTURE
2 Corinthians 7:1–16
Matthew 3:1–12

FOCUS
'Godly sorrow brings repentance that leads to salvation and leaves no regret, but worldly sorrow brings death.'
(2 Cor. 7:10)

Real repentance

leads to

changed thinking

Session 2
Relationship –
God in the driving seat

ICEBREAKER:
Write a prayer that tells God about your day – but in just three sentences.

FOR GROUP DISCUSSION/FURTHER THOUGHT:

- What is 'new' about your life now that you are a follower of Jesus?

- 'Prayer helps us to avoid self-centredness' – how?

- Have you had a crisis of obedience where you had to make a clear choice between what was right and what you wanted? How did it work out – and what did you learn?

- 'Prayer is a blessing to God' – how?

- Why do we struggle to simply be ourselves with God?

- What would some of the benefits of keeping a prayer journal be?

- How does the Bible 'feed' our relationship with God?

- What key truths about God have you learned on your Christian journey so far?

PRAYER:

Help me to share
my moments
and my days
with You,
Lord of life.
Amen.

Resources:

Jeff Lucas, *How not to pray* (Milton Keynes: Authentic Publishing, 2003)

All things new

BIG PICTURE
Revelation 21:1–5
2 Corinthians 5:17

FOCUS

'He who was seated on the throne said, "I am making everything new!" Then he said, "Write this down, for these words are trustworthy and true."' (Rev. 21:5)

IN THE celebrated and controversial film, *The Passion of the Christ*, a poignant scene (birthed in the screenwriter's imagination, but rooted in Revelation 21:5) unfolds when Jesus stumbles as He drags His cross along the Via Dolorosa. Mary, her heart shattered by the agony of a mother watching her child go to His execution, rushes to help Him to His feet and, as she does, she remembers a moment when He had a childhood scrape, and how she tenderly nursed Him. His face bloodied, Jesus gasps just one sentence to her, a few words that reveal the reason for the agony they share: 'You see, Mother, I'm making all things new!' It's a truth that Paul celebrates: 'Therefore, if anyone is in Christ, he is a new creation; the old has gone, the new has come!' (2 Cor. 5:17).

The call of Jesus is not a call to a patched-up existence but a renewed life, a renewed mind and a renewed lifestyle. This is radical stuff. When the first disciples bumped into Jesus, they signed up for a lifelong revolution. They made many mistakes still, but were on a totally new pathway. And, over the next few days, as we think about the value of obedience, the Bible, prayer and worship, it's because we want to live in that new life He promises.

Prayer: Thank You, Lord, that I now have hope, purpose, direction and new life in You. Continue to show me Your ways, in Jesus' name. Amen.

I AM constantly lost. I rather hope that this confusion is not genetically transmitted. When our grandchild, Stanley, was born, he was breech (chaps, that's upside down). This meant that a Caesarian section was necessary. Perhaps he's inherited my sense of direction, or lack thereof. Embarking on the short journey that is birth, there was only one way out – and he missed it.

Being lost on a car journey is horrible. Desperate, eventually I resort to pulling over and asking for directions. But then I get bored easily and so, while a willing stranger attempts to direct me with explicit instructions, my eyes glaze over and I fight sleep. For some reason, I seem to think that I know better. And then I get lost again.

And that's surely what gets a lot of us into trouble. As a new Christian, you have responded to Jesus' invitation to be one of His followers. Put simply, that involves listening to what He says about how to do life, and then doing it. Our obedience to Him demonstrates our growing love for Him.

God's commands are not friendly advice that we can take or leave. Moses didn't come down from Mount Sinai with the Ten Suggestions – they were orders. Whatever He says to you, do it. He really does know what's best for us.

Prayer: Lord, help me to obey You in everything. Amen.

Follow the instructions

BIG PICTURE
John 2:1–11
John 14:15–31

FOCUS
'His mother said to the servants, "Do whatever he tells you."' (John 2:5)

Whatever He says

to you, do it

15

The value of Scripture

BIG PICTURE
Acts 17:11–12
Hebrews 4:12–13

FOCUS
'Now the Bereans …
received the message
with great eagerness and
examined the Scriptures
every day to see if what
Paul said was true.'
(Acts 17:11)

CHRISTIANS believe that the Bible contains God's message to planet Earth. It's vital that your new-found faith is established on the truths of Scripture.

But that takes some care. If we don't learn how to use the Bible properly, we could think that adulterers should be stoned, slaves should be obedient rather than liberated, and life is all vanity anyway. Great damage has been done in history because the Bible was misused. The Bible describes itself as a sharp sword – and blades require diligent handling.

As Paul travelled to Berea, he discovered 'noble' people, noble because they examined the Scriptures daily to see if what he said was *true*. They didn't just *read* the Scriptures. The word Luke uses combines receptivity with critical questioning. The Greek verb for 'examine' is a judicial one, used to describe the cross-examination when Jesus was interrogated by Herod, and elsewhere. It speaks of thorough and intensive investigation – rather like good legal work. For the Bereans, this was not mere intellectual interest – their studying led to believing. God is not interested in us merely adding to our bank of information. He wants truth to change our lives and provoke faith.

As we come to Scripture, we wash our minds in truth, correct our skewed perspectives, and allow the 'sword' of the Scriptures to cut into our lives, confronting and cleansing us. Establish a daily habit of reading and reflecting upon Scripture. God has spoken to us through His Word. Let's listen.

Prayer: Teach me Your ways, that I might be changed as I discover Your Word of truth, Lord. Amen.

PRAYER – communicating with God – is essential to building our relationship with Him, but knowing how to do this isn't obvious. Even the twelve disciples of Jesus, who had observed His prayer life first-hand and were therefore in the best position to know how to do it, needed some extra help – 'Lord, teach us to pray', one of them asked. So, if we're struggling to know where to begin, let's not be discouraged.

God is a loving Father who already knows our needs (rather like a good parent) but wants us to share them with Him anyway. So we are invited to go to Him in conversation, asking Him to help us: as author Dallas Willard says, 'Request is at the heart of prayer'. Don't worry about asking too much – God encourages us to ask of Him. And don't get uptight trying to use the 'right' words: the correct way to pray is to say what's on your heart. As a new Christian I was delighted and excited to go to God with my needs, and those of others. I had a real anticipation about what God might do and saw some marvellous answers to prayer.

And listen up. God sometimes speaks, but when that happens, it's not usually through a loud voice from heaven, or writing in the sky … More often it's a quiet whisper, deep inside … or words that jump off the page … or a friend answers the question you've barely framed in prayer … Prayer is conversation. And conversation is the vital heart of any relationship, including our friendship with God.

Prayer: Lord, I want to grow closer to You. Teach me to share my life with You; help me to listen when You speak. Amen.

Prayer for beginners

BIG PICTURE
Luke 11:1–13
Romans 8:26–27

FOCUS
'… one of his disciples said to him, "Lord, teach us to pray …"'
(Luke 11:1)

… say what's on

your heart

Worship

Psalm 100
Romans 12:1–2

FOCUS
'Enter his gates with
thanksgiving and his
courts with praise …'
(Psa. 100:4)

'THANK you.' Just two words that mean so much
but, when missing, leave such a sour taste of
ingratitude. God has done so much for us – and
continues in His faithfulness every day. Thanks
(or thanksgiving) is certainly appropriate – and
that's one reason we worship.

Although worship is far more than singing (our
whole lives are to be an offering of worship),
finding a means of expressing our thanksgiving
and worship to God when alone and joining others
to praise God in prayer, song, liturgy, poetry and
art are vital. As we worship, we remind ourselves
that God is our number one priority; we celebrate
wonderful truths about Him as we sing and praise.
Worship enables us to focus on God and, as we
do, we have the opportunity to bring our lives into
realignment with His purposes. Sharing bread
and wine together reminds us once again of what
really matters: Christ has died; Christ is risen.
Christ will come again.

Worship is a way in which we express our love
for God. Just as in any relationship, sometimes
we will feel like expressing that love – and at other
times we won't. Don't worry about that – it's part
of being human. Worship anyway, because it's
right, and not just because it feels right.

God is worthy – that means He's worth
worshipping, whatever the weather.

**Prayer: Lord, teach me to worship You in all
things, with the whole of my life. Amen.**

Session 3
Community –
Fellow travellers needed

ICEBREAKER:

Think about your best friend. Describe him/her to others if you're in a group. If it's been a long-term friendship – why is that?

FOR GROUP DISCUSSION/FURTHER THOUGHT:

- What do you imagine are some of the joys of being part of a church – and what are some of the challenges?

- What do you think it means to be committed to the church?

- What do you see as being the difference between attending a church and belonging to one?

- What should our attitude be if we feel disappointed with church?

- What does a learner look like?

- How can we apply William Booth's phrase, 'Others', today?

- What are some of the characteristics of true friendship, and how can we build friendships with those qualities?

- Why might it be easy to become a spectator in church life? What might happen to us if we became one?

PRAYER:

May my church be stronger
because I am there, Lord.
Show me the part
You want me to play
for the purposes of Your kingdom.
Amen.

THE idea of being together as part of a community is very attractive. Television shows like *Cheers*, *Friends* and even *Coronation Street* all have this theme at heart; it's important to belong. But community is actually God's idea, and it's vital that we understand the purpose of the Church, the Christian community, which is far more than a religious club where like-minded people get together to sing and learn.

God's purposes on the earth have not been fulfilled through superstar individuals, but through a people. Throughout history, as God created a nation – Israel – in the Old Testament (and then another 'holy nation' – the Church of Jesus – in the New Testament), we see that His plan has always been for a community of people to be a lighthouse in the darkness. They would be a living demonstration of what it means to live life with God in charge. Christianity is not about 'flying solo' but rather 'formation flying'.

As we'll see (and you'll discover by experience), the Church is not perfect – nobody ever said it would be. The Church is an in-process, flawed, journeying people, just as we are. But being part of a church community is not an option for the Christian; it's the way God calls us to live – a family growing together in faith.

Prayer: Lord, thank You for the family of God, the Church. Bless the church of which I am a part. Thank You that I am not alone. Amen.

Together

BIG PICTURE
Ephesians 4:1–16
1 Corinthians
12:12–27

FOCUS
'From him the whole body, joined and held together by every supporting ligament, grows and builds itself up in love, as each part does its work.' (Eph. 4:16)

… a family

together growing

in faith

Belonging

BIG PICTURE
Romans 12:1–5
Acts 2:42–47

FOCUS
'... so in Christ we who
are many form one body,
and each member belongs
to all the others.'
(Rom. 12:5)

We belong

together, and to

each other

WE live in a consumer society, where we expect to get things our way (my coffee can now be made *exactly* to my liking). Unfortunately, there's also a danger that we become church 'consumers' too: unless the music is precisely to our taste and the sermon the right length (and peppered with humour) then we'll complain (or maybe go hunting for a church that will exactly hit the spot). But with that attitude we miss the point. Just as being part of a family is not about everyone orbiting around *my* needs, so church is not a product to be picky about.

Obviously we need to choose a church with a style and approach with which we feel compatible, but let's remember that we need our differences and our variety to function well together. The image of a body is one frequently applied to the Church (also known as the Body of Christ). Why? Well, just as the parts of a body look different, act differently and each has a different role and function, so do we. And that's the beauty of it. We all have our own unique contribution to make – from the smallest and youngest, to the oldest and (often!) wisest. So as you do what only you can do, everyone benefits. And that's what church should really be about.

So let's keep the consumerism for the cappuccino, and show commitment and loyalty to our church family. We belong together, and to each other.

Prayer: Lord, thank You for allowing me to be part of Your family. Save me from selfishness; help me to want to serve, and not just to be served. Amen.

JESUS repeatedly tells us to love one another, for the church family is to be where the unloved and the unlovely find acceptance, respect, dignity and unconditional love. But what does that mean in practice? Perhaps an episode from the life of William Booth, the founder of the Salvation Army, can help us. Asked to pen a telegram to be sent to stir and exhort the troops in his army around the world, and mindful of the high cost of international communications, he was keen to be economical with his words. In the end, he wrote just one word: 'Others' – so summing up the serving, selfless attitude to which the followers of Jesus must aspire: to put others before themselves. Not easy.

But look again at the context of Jesus' words in John 13 – He had just washed the disciples' feet, clearly demonstrating His love and tenderness towards each one of them. When we realise how much God loves us and learn to receive His love, we are better equipped to love and serve others from the overflow of that love. To constantly give out to others from our own resources, not drawing on God's infilling love, can be a recipe for discouragement or burnout.

So remember, our Servant King who washes the filthy feet of His friends wants us, His followers, to be just like Him, carrying His love way beyond the boundaries of the Church to the poor and broken of the world. 'Others' is a word for our lives in the Church – and outside it too.

Prayer: Lord, when I feel empty of love for those around me, help me not to give up – but to draw further on Your limitless love, and so continue to give and serve. Amen.

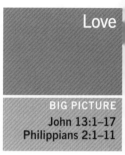

Love

BIG PICTURE
John 13:1–17
Philippians 2:1–11

FOCUS
'Now that I, your Lord and Teacher, have washed your feet, you also should wash one another's feet.'
(John 13:14)

Spectators

BIG PICTURE
Ephesians 2:1–10
Colossians 3:23–24

FOCUS
'For we are God's workmanship, created in Christ Jesus to do good works, which God prepared in advance for us to do.' (Eph. 2:10)

YESTERDAY I watched a panel of experts at a football match. They shouted when mistakes were made, and clapped and cheered when the solitary goal (for their team) was scored. They seemed to know exactly how the game should be played. There was just one problem: the only strenuous physical activity they engaged in during the match was collecting large slabs of pizza. They were experts. And spectators.

As you get involved in church life, you are not joining some multinational enterprise as a small anonymous cog in a very large impersonal machine. Nor are you there as a spectator – to watch everyone else perform. The Church is built on relationship and designed to be a family working together to see God's purposes fulfilled – and each family member has a unique role to play. We work and serve together out of love for God and for each other. Even though it is early days for you as a Christian, there are ways in which you can help. Don't just stand on the sidelines. It's harder work – but far more satisfying – to be involved rather than just observe. Volunteer to help out; don't be offended if you discover that there will be some tasks that those more mature in the faith have to handle. But do get your sleeves rolled up.

Prayer: Save me from becoming a spectator, Lord. Show me the role You have created for me to play. May my efforts make a difference in Your Church, and in Your world. Amen.

… do get your sleeves rolled up

IMAGINE a church with this reputation: some people believe in weird, unbiblical doctrines. Others claim to know Jesus but show up drunk at the meetings. Few respect the authority of the leaders. And then it's so cliquey – instead of being one united church, it seems to be split into a dozen factions. It's hard for newcomers to feel welcome and to know where they fit. Doesn't sound too inviting, does it?

But that's exactly the way the church in Corinth was two thousand years ago. It was large, growing fast – and a total mess. As a new Christian, you'll have high expectations of church. And that's good because when church is working well, newcomers are being loved and accepted, and hospitality, kindness and generosity shown, it can be the most healing, transforming and supportive place in the world to belong.

But, unfortunately, nobody's perfect and church is not always like that. And high expectations can also set you up for huge disappointment. Remember that church will be messy because it's made up of people who might have no reason to socially interact – except that, in finding Jesus, they've found each other. And it is filled with in-the-process humans. Those who are part of the Church are not there because they think they've arrived – on the contrary, they have realised that they need God's rescue. The Church is not a gleaming trophy case, it is a field hospital in the middle of a battlefield. Don't be amazed when people fail. We're good at that.

Prayer: Father, may Your Church reflect You – and may I do the same. Amen.

Messy church

BIG PICTURE
1 Corinthians 1:1–3
1 Corinthians 11:17–22

FOCUS
'When you come together, it is not the Lord's Supper you eat, for as you eat, each of you goes ahead without waiting for anybody else. One remains hungry, another gets drunk.'
(1 Cor. 11:21–22)

Session 4
Growth –
Are we nearly there yet?

ICEBREAKER:
What are some of your daily habits and routines?

FOR GROUP DISCUSSION/FURTHER THOUGHT:

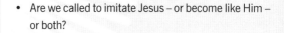

- What does a mature Christian look like?

- Are we called to imitate Jesus – or become like Him – or both?

- What disciplines do you think you might find helpful in your everyday life?

- What are some of the glaringly obvious bits of the 'old you' that have changed?

- How can we keep our minds healthy?

- Does faith including thinking, questioning and doubting?

- Why do some people turn their Christianity into a set of rigid rules and regulations rather than enjoying a daily friendship with God?

PRAYER:

Help me to choose
the patterns of my daily life
in a way that pleases You, Lord.
Amen.

Resources:
Richard Foster, *Celebration of Discipline* (London: Hodder & Stoughton, 2008)

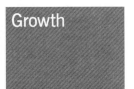

Growth

FOCUS
'But grow in the grace and
knowledge of our Lord
and Saviour Jesus Christ.
To him be glory both
now and for ever! Amen.'
(2 Pet. 3:18)

I AM currently on a diet (I have been for a decade). I am tracking my progress on my phone, which monitors my progress against the specific target weight I've set. The pancakes and syrup this morning didn't help.

As we think for the next few days about growing as a Christian, one vital question is: What does a 'grown-up' Christian look like? If we are to aim for growth, we need to have a target – an idea of what we are aiming to become. Sometimes people talk about becoming more 'spiritual' as they grow in Christ, but that can give the impression that God wants us to leave our humanness behind. That kind of thinking means that we feel good about prayer, worship, Bible study and attending Christian gatherings, but believe a round of golf, a walk on the beach or a meal with friends is suspect. But the truth is that God wants us to grow into being healthily human. Humanity is His idea – He invented the human race! And the ultimate picture of what healthy humanity looks like is Jesus. God wants us to know Him, and become like Him.

And so characteristics like love, kindness, generosity, serving, faith: all of these are evidence of authentic growth happening in our lives. Knowing God, and loving more: these are the ultimate signs of maturity.

Prayer: Lord, may today be a day of growing as a follower of Yours, as a friend to others, and as a healthy human being. Amen.

Knowing God,

and loving more

I am perhaps the world's worst gardener. I've never been able to produce anything much beyond a crop of prize-winning weeds. But even I know this much: I can plant seeds – yet I can't make them grow. Nature has to lend a helping hand and bring on the rain. Unfortunately nature only seems interested in the nettles in my back garden.

For the Christian, growth does not come about simply by our trying harder. The Christian life is not *just* about us doing the right kinds of things, but rather we need to be transformed each day into renewed people, who naturally do the right things because we are keeping in step with the Holy Spirit's activity in our lives. 'Just do better' is not the summary of Christian faith. 'Become better and changed by walking with God today' is the more biblical encouragement. Without the work of God's Spirit in our lives, nothing is achieved; nobody is transformed (John 15:5).

But, as we'll see tomorrow, that doesn't mean that we have no responsibility for the process of growth. As we learn to pray, reflect, be quiet, ponder and apply the Bible, we offer ourselves to the God who brings growth.

As we walk with God by faith through good and bad days, asking for His wisdom, trusting Him in storms, obedient and faithful – and getting up when we fall – so we grow. Ask God to fill you with His Holy Spirit today, and every day.

Prayer: Fill me with Your Spirit, Lord; change me, mature me, empower me. Amen.

By the Spirit

BIG PICTURE
Galatians 5:16–26
Ephesians 5:15–18

FOCUS
'But the fruit of the Spirit is love, joy, peace, patience, kindness, goodness, faithfulness, gentleness and self-control.' (Gal. 5:22–23)

Discipline

BIG PICTURE
1 Corinthians 9:24–27
Philippians 3:12–14

FOCUS
'No, I beat my body and make it my slave so that after I have preached to others, I myself will not be disqualified for the prize.' (1 Cor. 9:27)

YESTERDAY we saw that we can't just change ourselves, we need God's Spirit at work in us. But we do have a part to play. As I write this now, I am wrestling with my need to go to the gym for an hour. Even though I decided to run and lift weights regularly some six years ago, I still have to make what is often an irksome choice to do it daily. I also want to take some time to sit quietly and read the Bible. As an activist, it's easier for me to just dash on into my day.

Listening to Paul talking about making his body 'his slave', it's clear that growth only happens when we take tough choices about the way that we live. What our body demands may be compelling, but our bodies are not to be in charge of us. We are to be in charge of them.

The world was captivated when Michael Phelps took eight gold medals during the Beijing Olympics. But he achieved those dizzy heights by hard work and making his body his slave. In peak training phases, he swims at least 80,000 metres a week, nearly 50 miles. That includes at least two practices a day.

All that work was done for a temporary reward. One day the impressive row of medals will mean nothing, whereas Paul reminds us that we are in a race that affects eternity. Being a disciple involves being disciplined.

Prayer: Lord, help me to make good, daily choices about my life patterns and habits, and so co-operate with Your work in me. Amen.

Being a disciple

involves being

disciplined

TALKING about discipline means that we have wandered into a vital but dangerous subject. Whenever we set goals for our lives, we can end up creating lots of little laws, for ourselves and others. We start to believe, for example, that God will like us less if we don't pray for a certain amount of time. God might show us that a certain type of behaviour is not good for us personally (totally abstaining from alcohol is always going to be right for someone with a specific problem in that area), but before long we start to condemn others because they don't follow the same rules of life and faith that we do.

Some churches have been hijacked by this type of thinking. Lots of irrelevant regulations that go beyond what Scripture specifically asks of us are set in place and become the sign that we are really committed to Christ. This has always been a problem for the Church; how quickly we who have been freely set free by the shed blood of Christ meander back into following rules and regulations.

You are not saved and loved by God because you are always disciplined and pure; you are saved because of His great love and *what Jesus did for us all*. That love leads us to make disciplined choices – but our disciplines don't lead to God loving us more or less. Likewise, failure doesn't lessen God's love for you.

Prayer: Lord, thank You for all that You have done. Save me from straying into thinking that I can somehow earn Your love by my own efforts. Amen.

Freedom and legalism

BIG PICTURE
Galatians 5:1–13
Colossians 2:6–23

FOCUS
'It is for freedom that Christ has set us free. Stand firm, then, and do not let yourselves be burdened again by a yoke of slavery.' (Gal. 5:1)

Thinking about faith

FOCUS
'So I tell you this, and insist on it in the Lord, that you must no longer live as the Gentiles do, in the futility of their thinking.' (Eph. 4:17–18)

MEDITATION is a word that tends to conjure up images of an ethereal-looking person sitting, cross-legged, reflecting on the universe. But, as Christians, it's important that we learn to meditate – to think carefully – about God, about our lives and about what we believe. It's vital that we question, investigate and think about our faith, rather than accept a fill-in-the-blank Christianity that others spoon-feed us. Jesus constantly provoked questions; He didn't just make announcements of truth, but nudged those who were seeking truth to wrestle with challenging ideas.

Thinking Christianly is not just what Christians happen to think about things – because we can be wrong, as history has repeatedly proven. There was a time when 'Christian thinking' (the popular Christian consensus) was that slavery was acceptable. (We touched on that in Session 2: Day 3.) William Wilberforce and others brought that outrageous notion into question. And then Christian thinking is never noncommittal; it is not vague; our thinking leads us to action.

Don't just accept that what others tell you about faith must be true. Ask God to help you to use the mind He has given you. Take time to reflect on your journey; consider starting a journal; and never be afraid to ask questions.

… never be afraid

to ask questions

Prayer: Lord, I want to submit my mind to You; teach me to be still, to reflect, to think. Amen.

Session 5
Persistence –
Rough road ahead

ICEBREAKER:

Consider or share with others the toughest time of your life so far. What got you through?

FOR GROUP DISCUSSION/FURTHER THOUGHT:

* Why do people of faith suffer along with everyone else?

* Why do we instinctively want to believe that people of faith will be spared suffering?

* Is it all right to have unanswered questions?

* How can we help each other through the tough days?

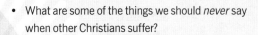

- What are some of the things we should *never* say when other Christians suffer?

- Is doubt normal? How do you deal with doubts?

- Why do some people get angry with God when life is tough?

PRAYER:

In the most difficult seasons of life,
help me to bring my doubts and unanswered questions
honestly before You.
May I be found faithful,
faithful God.
Amen.

Resources

Michael Baughen, *The One Big Question – The God of Love in a World of Suffering* (Farnham: CWR, 2010)

IT'S a television show that has taken Britain by storm. *The Apprentice* sees a number of assorted hopefuls compete for an opportunity to work for multimillionaire Lord Alan Sugar. But the television show isn't really about apprenticeship at all. An apprentice is invited on a journey with a master, to watch what they do and emulate it. Lord Sugar doesn't go anywhere, except to the boardroom and to a few locations where he gives his instructions. But Lord Sugar does want to 'hire' team players, even if the process of finding them involves some bristling competitiveness. And he's relentless: mess up, and you may face the pointed finger and hear the ominous words: 'You're fired!'

Jesus was a rabbi with apprentices. Like the other rabbis of His day, He invited His disciples to join Him on a training scheme that wasn't contained in the cloisters or the traditional classroom. Quite unlike the rabbis of His day, Jesus did not wait for applicants to come to Him but He chose them – and they were not the cream of the crop but just ordinary working men.

But His choosing of them was a great sign of hope. A rabbi's call meant that he actually believed that the chosen one could fulfil the apprenticeship. Jesus believes in us. And He doesn't just send us out but comes with us, by His Spirit. That's good news for today. Whatever may come, Jesus wants us on His team and promises that we'll never, ever, be alone again.

Prayer: Thank You, Lord, for 'taking me on' as Your apprentice. Teach me more about You today. Amen.

God has confidence in you

BIG PICTURE
John 15:1–17
Matthew 4:18–22

FOCUS
'You did not choose me … I chose … and appointed you to go and bear fruit … that will last. Then the Father will give you whatever you ask in my name.'
(John 15:16)

… we'll never,

ever be

alone again

Faith and suffering

BIG PICTURE
2 Corinthians 6:1–13
John 16:33

FOCUS
'Rather, as servants of God we commend ourselves in every way: in great endurance; in troubles, hardships and distresses.' (2 Cor. 6:4)

THERE are some Christians who insist that if we have enough faith we can avoid suffering. After all, we, the champions of faith, are the King's kids and if our loving heavenly Father (who is rich beyond compare) really cares about us, and if we stick close to Him, then surely we'll enjoy the best and escape pain, won't we? The notion is that we can always expect to be rich and pain-free.

Wrong. Very wrong. Paul had plenty of faith. And yet look at the lists of the trials and tribulations he went through. Right away we see that he didn't escape or avoid them and he was honest about the reality of them. Apparently Paul was also battling 'we triumph while others suffer' teaching in Corinth (hence his use of the word 'triumphal' in 2 Corinthians 2:14).

But he was unafraid to list the terrible experiences he'd had – in fact his times of suffering for the gospel are presented like authentic credentials. In what looks like weakness, he actually demonstrates true faith and trust. (Come to think of it, some of the greatest people of faith I've met have been confined to hospital beds.)

If you're suffering, don't let anyone tell you that you must be out of God's will or lacking in faith. Paul suffered. And he really was a champion.

Prayer: In suffering as well as blessing, may I be found faithful, Lord. Amen.

IF you have a pulse, you'll be tempted. What entices you may have no attraction for me – we're all different. But just as Paradise was blighted by temptation, so we will have to battle it in our everyday lives. There is a force of evil at work (in fact, we are living our lives in a spiritual battleground – see Ephesians 6:10–18) and the agenda is to drag us into the rebellion and madness of sin.

Notice the tactics of the tempter in this episode. First of all the serpent exaggerates the command of God, suggesting that He had said all the fruit in the garden was off-limits to the first couple. But that was a lie. Temptation can be strong when we feel overwhelmed, when we lose hope because we worry that what God asks of us is too much. That's why legalism (where rules that do not come from God are created) is so dangerous. When legalism overwhelms, people give up and, ironically, more sin results from their despair. And it's possible that exaggeration was also implied in Eve's statement, 'We must not eat of the fruit or even touch it' – but God did not say that either. It was only eating the fruit that was forbidden.

God wants us to be able to say 'No', not because He's a killjoy, but because He really does know what's best for us. When temptation comes, it comes with twisted promises and lies. Don't fall for it today.

Prayer: Lord, help me, in the fight of faith, to know truth and see through the false promises of deception. Amen.

Temptation

BIG PICTURE
**Genesis 3:1–24
1 Corinthians 10:12–13**

FOCUS
'The serpent was more crafty than any of the wild animals the LORD God had made. He said to the woman, "Did God really say, 'You must not eat from any tree'?"'
(Gen. 3:1)

If you have a
pulse, you'll
be tempted

Faith can bring pressure

BIG PICTURE
Luke 5:27–32
John 15:18–27

FOCUS
'… and Levi got up, left everything and followed him.' (Luke 5:28)

SOMETIMES I feel as though I need therapy before switching on the television news. The daily arrival of yet more apocalyptic headlines wearies me. But here's some encouragement: the Bible was written mostly to people who were battling with persecution, exile, economic turbulence and a myriad of other struggles. It's a vitally relevant message to people under pressure.

We've already seen that Christians are not exempt from pressure – and some of us are experiencing greater stress because we are followers of Christ. That was Matthew's (Levi's) experience. A well-heeled, fat-cat tax collector with a big income, he had endless resources; 'a large crowd' came to the meal he provided to honour Jesus and Luke tells us that it was a 'great' banquet. But now Matthew walks away from security and luxury because he wants to be an apprentice of the Rabbi Jesus. And while the fishermen in Jesus' team occasionally went back to fishing, Matthew never returned to his dubious trade. For him, in a sense, Jesus ushered in a massive credit crunch.

Sometimes being a follower of Jesus doesn't relieve pressure but increases it. And if we're in any doubt about that, consider the thousands of persecuted Christians around the world who are suffering bravely because of their love for Christ.

Prayer: Lord, when following You is costly and painful, help me to be faithful. Strengthen and bring hope to those who suffer for Your name. Amen.

SOMETIMES Christians use language that makes it sound as though God speaks to them directly daily, and they seem oblivious to any possibility of doubt. But doubts are actually very normal. We call each other 'believers' which means that faith is required to live the Christian life. There are times when our emotions are low, when difficult questions threaten to overwhelm us, or disappointment with other Christians can nag at our faith. Doubt can gnaw at us when we are asking God about something – and He appears to be silent. And when others seem to be walking through seasons of massive blessing, but the landscape of our lives feels barren, then doubt can loom once more. And doubt can send us spiralling down – as we wonder whether we are the only ones who have these troubling thoughts.

Don't be surprised when doubts come. And don't feel guilty because you experience them. Thomas had spent three whole years walking and talking with Jesus, but still struggled. Your feelings are not the barometer of your spirituality; they come and go. One day you will see Jesus face to face, and all possibility of doubt will be banished forever. In the meantime, if you doubt sometimes it doesn't make you a bad Christian – it just indicates that you aren't dead yet!

Prayer: Increase my faith, Lord. When times of doubt come, strengthen me; help me to trust in You. Amen.

Doubt

BIG PICTURE
James 1:2–8
John 20:24–31

FOCUS
'But when he asks, he must believe and not doubt, because he who doubts is like a wave of the sea, blown and tossed by the wind.' (James 1:6)

Don't be

surprised when

doubts come

SESSION 6
Purpose –
Where on earth are we going?

ICEBREAKER:
What are some of the most pressing needs of your community? Think about them – or discuss with others.

FOR GROUP DISCUSSION/FURTHER THOUGHT:
- How can we find out what our gifts are?

- What is the kingdom of God?

- 'We can't do everything – but we can all do something to change the world.' What does that mean for you?

- What would you say to a person who insists that Christianity should focus on getting people to heaven when they die, rather than changing the world here and now?

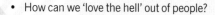

- How can we 'love the hell' out of people?

- How can we share our faith with others in a way that is helpful?

- 'Every community should be a better place because Christians live there' – do you agree?

PRAYER:

Help me
through the power of Your Spirit within me
to make a difference
in Your world today, Lord.
Amen.

Purpose and guidance

BIG PICTURE
Romans 12:1–2
Isaiah 6:1–8

FOCUS
'Do not conform any longer to the pattern of this world, but be transformed by the renewing of your mind. Then you will be able to test and approve what God's will is.'
(Rom. 12:2)

THE other day I watched a tightrope walker at work. The concentration on her face, with what looked like a hint of real fear in her eyes, made me glad that I didn't take the career path (or rope!) that she has taken.

I used to think that following Jesus was like walking a tightrope, and that finding out His will and purpose for my life was difficult and dangerous. What if I took a wrong turn? What if I made a huge mistake – would my life be useless and ruined?

A Christian is someone who wants to follow God's purposes for their life – but the best way to do that is to relax. Stop endlessly looking for God's guidance, and look for God Himself, as you think, pray, reflect and worship. Offer yourself willingly to God – our availability is the biggest key. God looked for a willing volunteer, and found him in Isaiah. Take advice from other trusted believers. Ask God not only to speak to you, but also to grow wisdom in you so that you will increasingly make wiser choices. Get to know Scripture. We make thousands of decisions where there is not a clear biblical answer to direct our choice – but there are many where God has already clearly revealed in His Word what He wants. An increasing sensitivity to what the Bible says will bring greater wisdom.

Prayer: Lord, I offer my moments, my days, my life to You and to Your purposes. Guide me in the way that I should go. Amen.

AS you grow in faith, you will discover areas of interest and concern where you will feel that you want to get involved, to change the world. But when we start to develop a strong sense of calling, there's a danger afoot. 'Calling wars' can break out. Suddenly we start to wonder why everyone else in our church doesn't feel as strongly about those things we feel passionate about – and conflict results. Those who feel that prayer is especially vital get irritated with those who are really committed to social action. Why are the social action people not spending more time seeking God? But then the social action people can see the praying people as vague, impractical airheads who need to stop praying and get on with feeding the poor. And so it goes on. Suddenly, the wonderful gift of diversity has become the primary source of conflict.

Let's realise that we're all different by design and respect each other's callings. When others don't share the same passion as us, it's not necessarily because they don't care as they should, but because they are wired differently. And God has done the wiring! Like an orchestra with a huge number of differently shaped and tuned instruments, we can get the job done as we co-ordinate, work together, play our part in harmony under God's direction, and faithfully share our gifts.

Prayer: Show me Your purposes for my life, Lord; and, when You do, may I be grateful for the concerns and callings You give to others. Amen.

Gifted

BIG PICTURE
1 Corinthians 12:12–31
Romans 12:6–8

FOCUS
'If the whole body were an eye, where would the sense of hearing be? If the whole body were an ear, where would the sense of smell be?' (1 Cor. 12:17)

God has done the wiring!

God's heart for justice

FOCUS

'Then the word of the LORD came to Elijah the Tishbite: "Go down to meet Ahab king of Israel … He is … in Naboth's vineyard … he has gone to take possession of it."'
(1 Kings 21:17–19)

GOD loves His world. And He calls us to do the same, which means that the plight of the poor matters. It's not just that charity is called for. God cries over the injustices that are created by greedy systems, corporations and governments. And caring for the environment is vital; we Christians believe that we don't own the planet. God made the world; It's only been lent to us. Justice in God's world, care for God's creation – these matter to God.

We can get overwhelmed by the sheer scale of the needs of our world, and even think that concern for the poor is more about politics and government than faith. But we are quite wrong if we try to escape the call to seeing our world changed. Nathan confronts King David about his treatment of poor Uriah (2 Sam. 12:9), and Elijah challenges King Ahab and Jezebel, his wife, over the way they snatch Naboth's vineyard away.

Jim Wallis describes a graphic illustration of just how much the Bible has to say about the poor – and what happens if we remove God's care for the poor from the Bible we teach:

A student took a Bible and cut out every reference to the poor with a pair of scissors. 'When the seminarian was finished that old Bible hung in threads. It wouldn't hold together, it fell apart in our hands. This is our Bible – full of holes.'

We can't do everything. But we can do something. And act we must.

Prayer: Lord, Your Word is plain: holiness without care for the poor is not holiness. Show me my part, that my world might be better. Amen.

NOW that you've become a Christian, it's natural that you'll want to share your faith with others. But that can seem a little awkward. Perhaps we've all felt uncomfortable as we've walked past that strange-looking man who shouts at people on the street corner. We don't want to turn into obnoxious 'Bible-bashers'.

We don't have to. Be natural in the way you talk about Jesus; He's a huge part of your life now. Aim to share your journey rather than win an argument. It's unlikely that you've developed 'religious' language yet – but beware! Often the best way to share Christ is by explaining what has happened to you, as people ask questions. Don't feel that every conversation has to lead to a conversion. It's our job to live beautifully with God's help and leave the results to Him. Pushing someone to make a decision is both rude and potentially unhelpful. Jesus invited people to count the cost before they decided to take the plunge and follow Him. We can't 'convert' anyone – that's God's job.

If you're asked a question and don't know the answer, say so. Listen to the views of others with respect. Invite others to come and see the church you're a part of. It can be helpful for them to see Christians worshipping, learning and doing life together.

Prayer: Lord, may my life and my words speak well of You, that others might discover You through me and through Your people. Amen.

Evangelism

BIG PICTURE
1 Peter 3:15–17
1 Corinthians 13:1–3

FOCUS
'Always be prepared to give an answer to everyone who asks you to give the reason for the hope that you have. But do this with gentleness and respect.'
(1 Pet. 3:15)

We can't 'convert' anyone – that's God's job

Ongoing change

BIG PICTURE
Romans 12:1–2
2 Corinthians 3:17–18

FOCUS
'And we, who with unveiled faces all reflect the Lord's glory, are being transformed into his likeness with ever-increasing glory … from the Lord, who is the Spirit.' (2 Cor. 3:18)

… you can

and will change

IT'S a saying that sounds so true: 'You can't get a leopard to change his spots.' In other words, what we are is what we are. We are stuck with sameness. Popeye the sailorman lamented his condition when he wailed: 'I yam what I yam.' All of which is desperate news, especially if we are addicted, fearful, destructive or angry. We can feel that our behaviour is inevitable and there is nothing to be done. But it's not true.

The Christian life is a life of gradual change, as we are transformed day by day by the work of God's Spirit in our lives. We increasingly take on the likeness – the character – of Jesus. We have to cooperate – and that means admitting we need help. Praying that God will change us is the first step.

It's a lifelong journey. Don't get discouraged when you fail – get up, accept God's forgiveness, and determine to keep following Him. If there are areas of your life where you feel stranded or stuck, or addictions that need to be broken, talk to another trusted Christian about them. As a Christian, you have not come to the conclusion that you're perfect – in fact it's the opposite – you've faced your need for Christ in your life.

Know this as you continue your journey: you can and will change, and for the better!

We follow Jesus. Not Popeye.

Prayer: Lord, as I continue a lifelong journey with You, cause me to change and grow, to be more like Jesus. Amen.

Wise words for a wild world

Lucas on Life Every Day brings you challenging Bible-application notes by well-known author and speaker, Jeff Lucas.

Published bimonthly, these probing and encouraging notes featuring Jeff's distinctive blend of passion, humour and insight will help you apply the Bible to your life every day.

ISSN: 1744-0122
£2.75 each (plus p&p)
£14.95 UK annual subscription (six issues)

To see our complete range of Jeff Lucas DVDs, Bible-reading notes and books, visit www.cwr.org.uk/lucas

Prices correct at time of printing

Courses and seminars

Publishing and new media

Conference facilities

Transforming lives

CWR's vision is to enable people to experience personal transformation through applying God's Word to their lives and relationships.

Our Bible-based training and resources help people around the world to:
• Grow in their walk with God
• Understand and apply Scripture to their lives
• Resource themselves and their church
• Develop pastoral care and counselling skills
• Train for leadership
• Strengthen relationships, marriage and family life and much more.

CWR Applying God's Word
to everyday life and relationships

CWR, Waverley Abbey House,
Waverley Lane, Farnham,
Surrey GU9 8EP, UK

Telephone: **+44 (0)1252 784700**
Email: **info@cwr.org.uk**
Website: **www.cwr.org.uk**

Registered Charity No 294387
Company Registration No 1990308

Our insightful writers provide daily Bible-reading notes and other resources for all ages, and our experienced course designers and presenters have gained an international reputation for excellence and effectiveness.

CWR's Training and Conference Centre in Surrey, England, provides excellent facilities in an idyllic setting – ideal for both learning and spiritual refreshment.